FEMALE FIGURE SKATING LEGENDS

Oksana Baiul

Nicole Bobek

Ekaterina Gordeeva

Nancy Kerrigan

Michelle Kwan

Tara Lipinski

Katarina Witt

Kristi Yamaguchi

CHELSEA HOUSE PUBLISHERS

OKSANA BAIUL

Lonnie Hull DuPont

CHELSEA HOUSE PUBLISHERS
Philadelphia

Produced by Choptank Syndicate, Inc.

Editor and Picture Researcher: Norman L. Macht
Production Coordinator and Editorial Assistant: Mary E. Hull
Design and Production: Lisa Hochstein

CHELSEA HOUSE PUBLISHERS

Editor in Chief: Stephen Reginald
Managing Editor: James Gallagher
Production Manager: Pamela Loos
Art Director: Sara Davis
Photo Editor: Judy L. Hasday
Senior Production Editor: Lisa Chippendale
Publishing Coordinator: James McAvoy
Cover Illustration: Keith Trego

Cover Photos: front cover, right, and back cover: AP/Wide World Photos;
             front cover, left: Lee/Archive Newsphotos

The Chelsea House World Wide Web site address is
http://www.chelseahouse.com

First Printing

1 3 5 7 9 8 6 4 2

Library of Congress Cataloging-in-Publication Data

DuPont, Lonnie Hull.
    Oksana Baiul / Lonnie Hull DuPont.
     p.   cm. — (Female figure skating legends)
    Includes bibliographical references and index.
    Summary: A biography of the young Ukrainian figure skater who
won a gold medal at the 1994 Winter Olympics.
    ISBN 0-7910-4201-4 (hc)
    1. Baiul, Oksana, 1977 or 8- —Juvenile literature. 2. Skaters—
Ukraine—Biography—Juvenile literature. [1. Baiul, Oksana, 1977 or 8- .
2. Ice skaters. 3. Women—Biography.] I. Title. II. Series.
GV850.B35D87   1998
796.91'2'092—dc21   98-21901
    [b]   CIP
                                                                    AC

CONTENTS

GOING FOR THE GOLD

In February 1994, flanked by coaches Galina Zmievskaya and Valentine Nicolaj, Oksana Baiul flew to Lillehammer, Norway, for the winter Olympics. The dream of her life was about to unfold before her. But her excitement was muted by the absence of her mother, who had died when Oksana was 14.

A source of encouragement at all times, her mother had told Oksana that whatever happened, she would be with her daughter, and Oksana believed it.

The press, who had before been so fascinated by the brooding yet sparkling Ukrainian girl who told them she skated to forget the pain in her life, now switched its fascination to the stories of two all-American skaters who were so different from one another—clean-cut

Oksana finishes her short program at the 1994 Olympics in Norway. Fulfilling her late mother's wish, she skated to Tchaikovsky's Swan Lake.

Nancy Kerrigan and wild Tonya Harding. Nancy had been attacked by an unkown assailant at the 1994 Nationals in Detroit, and recently Tonya had been implicated in the scandal. Since there was no proof yet against Tonya, the USFA let her go to the Olympics. The showdown between the two American skaters caused an unprecedented number of people to watch the Olympic skating competitions. Cameras and microphones constantly trailed them through the Olympic Village.

Oksana liked the media attention, but she also knew she needed to stay focused at the Olympics. She could see her competition clearly, and one of her toughest competitors was going to be Nancy, in spite of her wounded knee. Oksana understood fully that a skater could rally from something painful and frightening to skate something great, and that is exactly what Nancy might do. Oksana needed to stay steady and work hard until it was time to perform.

Competition had begun with the short program, in which Oksana skated to *Swan Lake*. She kept her mind trained on her movements and on Galina's advice: "Think only of becoming a swan on the ice."

Dressed in a sequined black costume to suggest a black swan, and wearing a feathered headpiece, Oksana touched her babushka's (grandmother's) gold cross around her neck and skated onto the ice. At first she skated around in a small circle. Galina had taught her not to rush, and Oksana took her time positioning herself. The crowd was hushed and expectant.

Oksana struck her opening pose, and the familiar strains from Tchaikovsky began. Besides her impressive technical work of jumps and speed, she used movement that suggested the actions of an elegant bird moving its wings

and flying low. She even moved to look like she was a swan bobbing its head on its long neck. The effect was captivating. The audience was riveted, and Oksana felt alive and full of energy.

At the end, when she folded onto the ice like the dying swan, the crowd cheered wildly. Oksana whispered to the ice, "I skated Swan Lake, Mama. I skated it for you."

Oksana placed second in the short program, just behind Nancy Kerrigan. The Ukrainian group in Lillehammer was thrilled. The next day, Oksana and her coach, Galina, went to the rink where six other skaters were practicing. Oksana worked on her jumps. Then the unthinkable happened: a mid-air collision on the ice between

Oskana's eyes pop open with delight and her coaches Galina Zmievskaya and Valentine Nicolaj are pleased as her short program scores are announced at the 1994 Olympics.

Oksana and Germany's Tanja Szewczenko. Katarina Witt, who later described it as one of the worst crashes she had ever seen, helped Oksana up first, then went to help her own teammate. The media cameras missed the accident completely.

Unfortunately, Tanja's skate had dug deeply into Oksana's lower leg, causing it to bleed. The fall itself had hurt Oksana's back, and she could tell her chronic disk problem was acting up again. Devastated, she limped over to Galina.

A German doctor examined the skater and put three stitches in her leg. The back pain was another thing. The doctor told her that it was a slipped disk, that by morning it would be worse, and that she might not be able to skate in the freestyle competition. Galina calmed her down, telling her that she could try the warm-up the next day, but if there was any pain, she could not compete.

Oksana was horrified. After all her working and dreaming, she was determined to compete at all costs. The rest of the day and evening, both coach and skater felt nervous, but at least they had a plan.

As the doctor had warned, the pain was severe the next day. At warm-up, Oksana was in so much pain she began to cry. Galina seemed stoic about it all. She, too, was disappointed, but she told Oksana that it was not right to sustain permanent injuries just for the sake of a sport. Anyway, Galina reminded her, there was always the next Olympics. Oksana left the rink and unlaced her skates. When she looked back at Galina, she saw that Galina, her tough coach, was crying, too.

Oksana decided that somehow she would skate that day. She went back to Galina and insisted on being allowed to compete. Galina finally gave in.

They asked the doctor to give Oksana two Olympic-approved injections for the pain. She was still in some pain, and she was queasy from the medication. But pain was nothing new to her. She practiced briefly, then left the ice to mentally prepare herself for the freestyle long program. She would need all the focus and energy she could muster.

The competition began. Nancy Kerrigan came just before Oksana in the lineup of performances, but Oksana stayed backstage during Nancy's performance and took her time getting into her shiny, feathery pink costume. She could hear from the cheering that Nancy had done well.

Oksana hugs Tanja Szewczenko after their on-ice collision during a practice session. Tanja's skate dug into Oksana's leg, which required stitches. With her injured back and leg, doctors doubted Oksana could finish competing in the 1994 Olympics.

Now it was Oksana's turn. She skated gingerly onto the ice, her injured leg feeling stiff at first. She recalled her coach's words: "Take your time." She recalled her mother's words: "I will always be with you." She gently limbered her spine, again grateful for the drug which at least took the edge off the pain. She stopped skating momentarily as the unusually high number of bouquets thrown to Nancy were scooped up from the ice by the skating flower girls.

Now it was time. The announcer spoke: "On the ice, representing Ukraine . . . Oksana Baiul."

Despite the pain of her injuries, Oksana Baiul skated a flawless long program, which included her signature spin, shown here. Oksana wore her grandmother's gold cross for good luck and placed first, becoming the first athlete to win a gold medal for the Ukraine.

She made the sign of the cross and struck her opening pose. The cameras watched. The world waited. She took a deep breath and said a quick prayer. The image of her dead mother flashed through her mind, and Oksana knew her mother was with her in spirit. Now Oksana was ready.

The medley of Broadway songs began, and Oksana took off, looking as if she were in no pain whatsoever, and landed her opening jump, the triple Lutz. She skated with tremendous drama and finesse, landing a triple loop, a Lutz, and a Salchow—a jump that starts from the back inside edge of the skate and lands backward on the outside edge of the opposite skate.

She skipped some important technical maneuvers at first as she tried to sense what her body could do in its impaired state. She dropped combination jumps and changed a triple toe loop to a double. But she felt relaxed and sensed the audience's enjoyment of her performance, which meant the most to her.

Near the end after her program, Oksana had to make a snap decision: should she continue to tone down her technical parts to favor her injuries or should she go for the gold? There wasn't much time to decide. "How much do I want to win?" she asked herself.

Quickly Oksana adjusted her program. She attempted another triple toe loop and landed it this time, followed immediately by a double Axel–double toe loop combination. It was daring, but it worked. She skated into her ending pose just as the music stopped.

The effect of this courageous finale on the audience was stupendous. The crowd roared as Oksana wept on the ice. Crying and beaming at the same time, she made her way over to her coach to wait for scores. "Your mama helped

*Gold medal winner
Oksana Baiul stands
with U.S. silver medalist
Nancy Kerrigan and
bronze medalist
Chen Lu of China
at the 1994 Olympics
in Lillehammer, Norway.*

you from up above," Galina whispered to Oksana as she gathered the shaking girl into her arms.

The competition ended in a tie for total scores between Oksana and Nancy Kerrigan. But Oksana's artistic scores were slightly higher than Nancy's and, under the rules, that tipped the balance in her favor.

The camera lightbulbs of the world press flashed and flashed on Oksana as her aqua eyes grew wide with disbelief, then wet with tears of joy. This was exactly what she had dreamed of—she had won the gold at the tender age of 16. "It was the happiest day of my life," she later claimed.

When the hysteria began to die down, officials scrambled to find the music for the

Ukrainian national anthem, and Oksana composed herself for the awards ceremony. Soon, flanked by silver medalist Nancy Kerrigan and bronze medalist Chen Lu, a happy Oksana stood with the Olympic gold medal around her neck and smiled as her nation's flag unfurled. The strains to "Ukraine Has Not Died" rose over the crowd, and Oksana moved her lips to the words.

Never before had the Ukrainian national anthem been played at an Olympics.

A Fairy Tale Begins

Oksana Baiul was born on November 16, 1977, in the Ukrainian factory town of Dnepropetrovsk, where nuclear missiles were manufactured. At the time of Oksana's birth, the Ukraine was one of 15 republics that made up the nation then called the Soviet Union. Later, when the Soviet Union collapsed and broke into 15 separate countries, Ukraine became an independent country.

Oksana's parents were Sergei and Marina Baiul. Oksana never actually knew her father, because he abandoned the family when she was only two years old. Her mother was the driving force in Oksana's childhood as well as her closest friend. Oksana had no brothers or sisters, and she and her mother shared their small three-room apartment with Oksana's

This woman wears the traditional dress of the Ukraine, where Oksana Baiul was born in 1977. While Oksana lived there, Ukraine—which achieved independence in 1992—was part of the former U.S.S.R.

grandparents. Housing shortages were common in the U.S.S.R., and it was not unusual for many people to share a tiny apartment. The three adults adored their little girl.

Because most of her childhood was spent with her grandparents and her mother, Oksana grew up seeming more mature than other children. Her wide blue-green eyes were somber, and she often wore a serious expression that made her appear wise beyond her years. But those who knew her were not fooled by this, because Oksana was great fun. She was a tomboy known for taking risks, an attitude that would serve her well on the ice.

Oksana's early years were secure and full of affection. Her mother loved to sew clothes for her and comb her long blond hair. While her mother worked as a French teacher in the local school, Oksana's grandmother—known in Russian as her babushka—took care of her, entertaining Oksana with stories. Her grandfather worked in a nearby park, and he, too, doted on his granddaughter when he came home at night.

When she was young, Oksana's mother, Marina Baiul, had been a dancer with high hopes of success. In the Soviet Union, dancers and athletes were held in high esteem, as high as famous scientists or writers or artists. Because dancers and athletes honored the country with their success, the U.S.S.R. encouraged them and provided funding for their training.

Marina was no longer a dancer, but she was certain Oksana could be one. Babushka filled Oksana's head with charming stories about her mother's dancing, and Oksana grew up seeing a side of her hard-working mother that inspired her from an early age. Tiny Oksana would

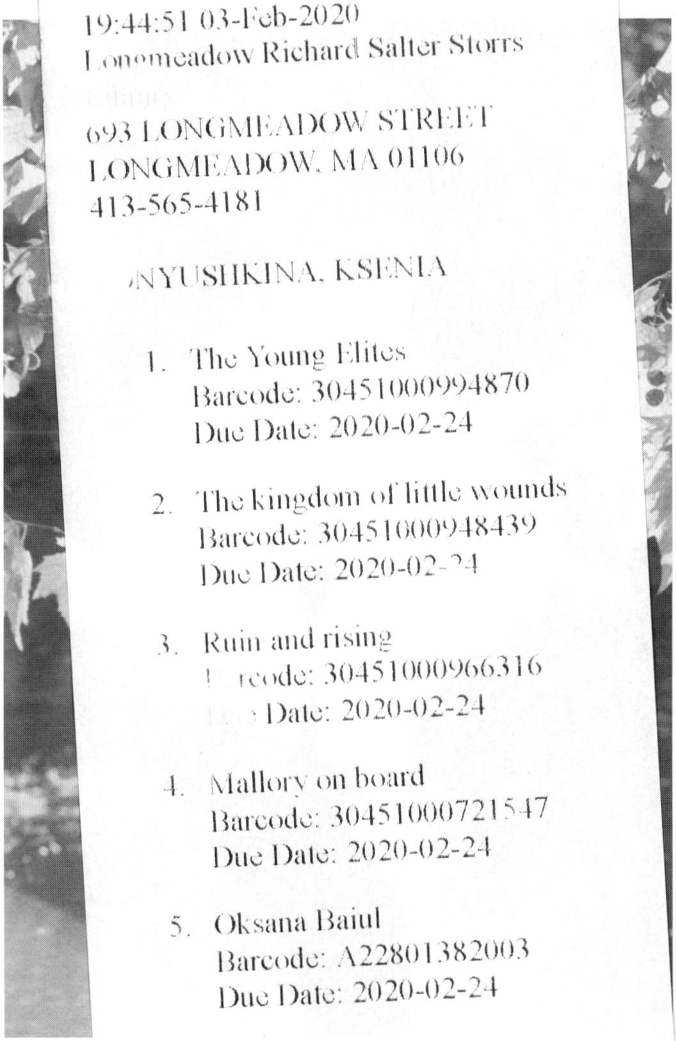

19:44:51 03-Feb-2020
Longmeadow Richard Salter Storrs

693 LONGMEADOW STREET
LONGMEADOW, MA 01106
413-565-4181

ONYUSHKINA, KSENIA

1. The Young Elites
    Barcode: 30451000994870
    Due Date: 2020-02-24

2. The kingdom of little wounds
    Barcode: 30451000948439
    Due Date: 2020-02-24

3. Ruin and rising
    Barcode: 30451000966316
    Due Date: 2020-02-24

4. Mallory on board
    Barcode: 30451000721547
    Due Date: 2020-02-24

5. Oksana Baiul
    Barcode: A22801382003
    Due Date: 2020-02-24

6. The language of thorns :
    midnight tales and dangerous
    magic
    Barcode: 30451001175198
    Due Date: 2020-02-24

7. Huntress
    Barcode: 304   0680
    Due Date: 2020-02-24

Oksana's mother, Marina Baiul, was a dancer, and her favorite ballet was Swan Lake, *shown here. Though Marina Baiul accepted that Oksana preferred skating to ballet, she always hoped that one day Oksana would skate to the music of* Swan Lake.

dance
much
applau
a beau
   Wh
decided
ballet c
self to
went out to get her enrolled. Instead he came home with a box under his arm. "No ballet school will take Oksana," he said, grinning. "She's too

young, and she's too fat. But don't worry—
I have brought a very special present for her."

Oksana opened the box. Inside were a pair
of ice skates. "Thank you, Grandfather," she
squealed happily.

Marina raised an eyebrow at her father. She
had hopes for ballet school. They were no poorer
or richer than their neighbors, but they certainly
could not spend money on unnecessary items.

"She should figure skate," Grandfather
explained. "It will trim her down for the ballet."
Marina saw the sense of that and nodded
her approval.

As for little Oksana, she couldn't be happier.
It didn't matter that the skates weren't new.
In fact, it would be years before she had
new skates. But these skates with their shiny
blades and smooth leather were nothing short
of beautiful to her.

The Soviet Union sent talented children to special sports schools, like this school for young gymnasts, where they could practice their sport from an early age and combine athletic training with traditional studies. Oksana attended a special skating school.

The next day, Oksana and her grandfather walked to the skating rink in town. She put on the skates and stepped out onto the ice. At four years old, she could skate immediately. She didn't even fall down.

"From the moment I stepped on the ice, I loved skating," she would later write. "Around me, the other kids slipped . . . and fell. Not me. I skated faster and faster. I never wanted to stop."

From then on, Oksana delighted in skating. The skating rink was always cold but she didn't care. Her mother and babushka bundled her up in layers of heavy sweaters and warm tights, and off they went.

It wasn't long before Oksana was doing far more than skating fast. Soon she was skating backwards and trying little hops into the air. She fell occasionally, but overall she was daring on the ice. It came as naturally to her as did dancing around the apartment.

Marina could see that her daughter was a born skater, but she continued to view skating as simply preparation for ballet. However, when Oksana was only five, one of the best coaches in the Ukraine noticed her talent and approached Marina.

Coach Stanislav Korytek trained his skaters at the rink where Oksana practiced, and he had been keeping his eye on the fearless little girl who seemed born to the ice. Convinced that Oksana had the makings of a champion, Korytek approached her mother and offered to coach Oksana. Marina was flattered, but she also knew the commitment involved if Oksana decided to work with a coach of such international fame in the skating world. It would mean daily practice, even when Oksana should be in school. And besides that, with her modest wages as a teacher, Marina knew she couldn't afford to pay for the coaching.

But Korytek reminded Marina that the Soviet government, in its dedication to fine athletes, would pick up the tab for most of the training. Korytek explained that there were even special schools for athletes where they could study and practice their sport. Marina was relieved to hear that Oksana's skating practice would not interfere with her studies, and she gave her consent for Korytek to work with Oksana to see if her talent could be developed.

So began the training. Every day Oksana hit the ice. She practiced spins, school figures, and crossovers, and she began to learn jumps. Soon she was skating better and stronger than ever. Although Korytek was a strict coach, he

Unlike many children, Oksana, shown here at the 1994 Olympics, could skate from the moment she first set foot on the ice.

became a father figure to Oksana and a very good friend as well. She called him Coach Stanislav. Oksana loved Korytek, and she loved the rigorous discipline of skating. She did not mind having to practice for hours each day while other children played outside. From the beginning, Oksana devoted herself to figure skating.

When Oksana turned seven, Coach Stanislav entered her in her first skating competition. Now she had a new feeling about skating—fear. For the first time, she felt apprehensive about going on the ice. Before it had been only fun— hard work, yes, but still fun. Now there were expectations.

On the day of the competition, Oksana put on her new bright green skating dress. It brought out the green in her troubled eyes.

Marina noticed her child was extremely quiet. "What's wrong?" she asked.

"I'm scared," Oksana said. "What if I fall down in front of everyone?"

"It won't matter," her mother said. "Remember what Coach Stanislav says. Always smile when you are on the ice, and have a good time. Then everything will be all right."

It was that advice and that first local competition that inspired a performance style for little Oksana. She learned to beam at the audience and enjoy her skating rather than worry about what bad things could happen. Coach Stanislav had taught her single jumps, then double jumps. She could even spin around twice in the air at the age of seven. She twirled like a dancer. And she didn't fall at her first competition; in fact, she won.

Afterward, a decision was in order in the Baiul household. The Soviet Union began training ballerinas at age seven, and now Oksana

At her very first skating competition, Oksana was afraid of falling. Here she lets her relief show after completing a perfect performance in 1994.

was the right age and she was in good physical shape to begin ballet school. Marina asked Oksana if she wanted to switch from skating to ballet.

"No," said Oksana firmly. "I want to keep on skating. I don't ever want to do anything else."

With her love of the ice and her first prize, Oksana never looked back. Eventually she would go to ballet school, but then it would be to enhance her skating instead of the other way around. Though it was not her first love, ballet was excellent training for figure skating. It taught Oksana grace and poise, and she learned how to interpret emotions in her performances on the ice.

Marina Baiul accepted her daughter's decision to pursue figure skating instead of ballet, despite her dream of watching Oksana become a famous dancer.

There was one ballet dream of Marina Baiul's, however, that Oksana absorbed from an early age. Marina's favorite ballet was *Swan Lake*. Now she put on a recording of it in the apartment and asked Oksana if she could skate to it.

"I can't, Mama," Oksana said. "The music is too slow. I want to skate to something I can do a lot of jumps to."

Her mother smiled. Even though dancing to *Swan Lake* was the dream of every ballerina, Marina knew her daughter was in perpetual motion and not inclined to slow down for anything, much less music by Tchaikovsky. Nevertheless, Marina said, "Someday you will understand the music, Oksana. Someday you will skate to *Swan Lake*."

THE DARKEST HOURS

Oksana's early childhood was a happy one. In the beginning, it was full of the love and attention of her family, and as time went by, it also became busy with school, skating lessons, and friends. Since most of the skaters in Dnepropetrovsk were boys, Oksana practiced with them. Her best friend was a boy skater named Slavik, and the two practiced with each other constantly, competing to outjump or outskate each other.

Oksana landed her first triple jump—a triple Lutz—when she was nine. The Lutz is one of the hardest jumps for most skaters. Oksana found it to be not only easy but fun. It became her favorite jump. Consequently, in the future, she would often perform a triple Lutz at the beginning of most of her programs.

No matter what tragedy or frustration plagued Oksana's life, she never gave up her love of skating.

It took longer for Oksana to perfect her double Axel, however. This jump is usually mastered before any triples. In the Axel, the skater takes off from a forward position on the outside edge of one skate, then rotates once (or twice for the double) with an extra half turn to enable her to land backward on the outside edge of the opposite skate. For some reason, this movement was more difficult for Oksana. She learned the triple Lutz before the double Axel.

In many ways, these early years were rich ones for Oksana. She barely noticed that life in the Ukraine was never easy. Oksana and the three adults who made up her family all lived in a small one-bedroom apartment, a normal living space for most Ukrainians. Shortages in items Americans take for granted such as meat, fresh produce, and even medicines were routine in the Ukraine.

Then in 1986 a national tragedy struck. In the Ukrainian town of Chernobyl, a nuclear power generator went out of control, sending vast quantities of lethal radioactivity into the open air. The sickness from this was rampant. In addition to the breakouts of illness and death, radioactivity rained down on the many huge fields of grain that fed most of the Soviet Union. The republic that geography books called "The Breadbasket to the World" now had extremely dangerous farming conditions. All over the country, life became more difficult than before.

In 1988 Oksana was hit with a personal tragedy when her grandfather died. A year later she lost her babushka. Oksana and her mother grieved deeply over these deaths. The little apartment seemed huge and terribly quiet without the grandparents. Oksana was given her babushka's gold cross necklace, which she put on and seldom took off. She would touch it for comfort from time to time.

Now Oksana and Marina were alone together, and their worlds revolved around one another. Marina continued to encourage Oksana to skate and was pleased that she was so skilled at it. Oksana's grief cast a cloud over her love of skating. She continued to work hard, but her joy was gone. One day she told her mother that she was through skating, and she quit. Marina worried, but she decided to let her daughter work it out by herself.

Now Oksana tried to be what she later called "a normal girl." But she missed skating so much that she felt her heart was breaking. "I liked [skating] more than my life," she would later say. After two weeks, she went back to the rink with even more resolve to be a superior skater.

Slavik and Oksana had watched the 1988 winter Olympics together on television. She was so thrilled with what she saw that her dream became skating in the Olympics. When she shared it with her mother, Marina told her, "You will be a great skater. I feel it in my heart. You must follow your dream." And she kissed her daughter.

With renewed passion, Oksana learned and improved her jumps, loops, and spirals. She put together short and long programs for competition. The two-minute short program is the technical one which must include certain jumps, spins, and footwork. The four-minute long program is a freestyle performance in which the skater highlights what she does best.

Oksana worked hard on her programs, entering local competitions or even performing for an audience of one at the rink if necessary, because now she had a definable goal. She didn't want simply to be good; she wanted to follow her idol, East German skater Katarina Witt, and stand on the Olympic stage receiving a gold medal.

In 1990 Oksana watched ice skating on television again, and she saw something different in Jill Trenary's performance. While every skater's performance highlighted her skills on ice, Jill's performance in addition showed grace

After the 1988 Olympics East German figure skater Katarina Witt became Oksana's idol.

and beauty, the elements of dance. From that moment on, Oksana began working not only on her technical aspects but on her creative presentation as well.

The year 1991 started on a positive note for Oksana when she competed at the U.S.S.R. Nationals. Out of all that nation's skaters—and the Soviet Union was a huge nation full of excellent skaters—Oksana placed 12th. This was an amazing accomplishment and a solid sign that she should continue her hard work.

But that year Marina became ill. She had always been a robust woman, and sickness was unusual for her. Now, however, at the age of 36, she was dying of a fast-spreading ovarian cancer. She gave Oksana one of Babushka's rings to wear as a reminder that Oksana should never feel that she was alone. It was evident that Marina was gravely ill, but death came much quicker than anyone expected. In August Oksana was skating at the rink when Coach Stanislav gently told her that her mother had died. Oksana was stunned and devastated. It was the hardest, saddest time of her life.

At the funeral, she sat alone, crying and bewildered. Her father, who had abandoned the family, was at the funeral. It was the first time Oksana had seen him since she was a toddler, but they did not speak. No relationship developed between father and daughter.

Marina had recently remarried, and Oksana's stepfather was kind, but Oksana hardly knew him. It was too painful to return to the apartment, so after the funeral she fled to the skating rink. That night, Coach Stanislav found her there "gliding and crying, crying and gliding." He convinced her to come live with him and his family. The Koryteks were very kind to the grieving girl.

More than ever before, Oksana threw herself into skating. It became the only time she felt alive and happy. Her life was full of muscular aches and pains from her hard, almost obsessive, skating work, and her mother was no longer there to console her. But Oksana fingered the ring on her hand and kept her mother in her heart and continued to skate.

Oksana and Coach Stanislav realized that she needed to compete more nationally to be in the running as a serious skater. So in November 1991 she entered an important competition in Moscow. She prepared with all her heart and might. Then without explanation, Coach Stanislav told her he could not go with her to Moscow. Oksana pleaded, but her coach insisted he could not attend the competition. "You will do fine without me," he said.

Without her coach or her mother to accompany her to such an important competition away from home in a large city, a terrified Oksana considered not going at all. But her friend Slavik saved the day and went with her.

Even though the stands were full of people in Moscow, Oksana knew exactly where Slavik sat. She smiled at him and thought of her mother. Then she skated onto the ice and performed flawlessly. The Ukrainian skater nobody had heard of glided away with the gold medal.

The next day, back in Dnepropetrovsk, a victorious Oksana ran to the skating rink to show Coach Stanislav her prize. But he was not in his office where he should be. She ran to his house, and he wasn't there either. After enduring a couple weeks of waiting for him, she learned that he had moved to Canada and taken another coaching job. He was never coming back.

This was another blow in the young girl's life, and she felt abandoned once again. On one level, she understood why he left. In August 1991 a political group had attempted unsucessfully to overthrow the government of the Soviet Union. Though the people went on with their lives, the Soviet government was in turmoil, and the economy was collapsing. By the end of 1991, the republics of the Soviet Union separated to become individual countries.

This government chaos meant that life was becoming impossible for a coach like Korytek whose work was sponsored by the government. The funding for his skaters and his livelihood became unpredictable. Oksana would later be gracious about it by saying, "Everyone wants to eat."

Oksana also understood why Coach Stanislav didn't confide in her that he was leaving. He didn't tell anybody. Soviet citizens had to be very secretive about moving out of the country. The government probably would have prevented his travel had they known he was not returning.

Life was complicated, and even more so in the Soviet Union in 1991. Oksana Baiul had lost not only her coach, but the father figure in her life in the same year she had lost her mother. She was truly alone now, and she became depressed.

Oksana left the Korytek apartment and moved in with her stepfather. She vowed never to skate again. She avoided the rink every time she left the apartment. She even threw her skates away.

After two weeks she knew that she needed to skate again. Fortunately, Slavik had rescued her skates from the trash, just waiting for her to come to her senses. "I knew you could never stop skating," he said.

Gratefully, Oksana began skating again. She worked herself hard without a coach.

During these months, with the housing shortages, Oksana had to leave the apartment she grew up in to make room for a family. She took very little with her. Sometimes she lived with her stepfather, whom she never really came to know very well, and sometimes she slept on a cot in the basement of the skating rink, getting herself up to wash and go to school. Then she'd come back and skate for hours.

At the beginning of 1992 the Ukraine became an independent nation. Life was harder for everyone. Jobs were scarce. People had to stand in long lines to buy the simplest items. Even bread was hard to get. But good things waited around the corner for one young Ukrainian and her dream.

FROM ODESSA
TO THE WORLDS

Now that Oksana was focused once again, she continued to compete, working alone. Daily life remained difficult. Like Oksana, the new nation of Ukraine was slowly and dramatically sorting itself out, learning how to exist independently.

As time went by, people in the skating world started talking about the young, talented skater named Oksana, who worked without a coach. The word about her reached Ukrainian skater Viktor Petrenko, an Olympic gold medalist in 1992, and he found a way to watch her skate.

Viktor was impressed, not only by her talent but by her gumption. He was engaged to the daughter of a skating coach, Galina Zmievskaya, and he approached his future mother-in-law to suggest she take Oksana as a student.

Not long after meeting Coach Galina Zmievskaya, Oksana received international attention and was invited to perform with the Campbell Soup Tour of World Figure Skating Champions.

Galina knew that any skater who worked with her would have to live in her hometown of Odessa so that they could train together daily. Moving to a strange town from Oksana's own home 250 miles away would be a big commitment for a young teen. "I have to speak to her parents first," Galina told Viktor.

"She has no one," he said.

Galina was stunned. Then she was moved. It was clear to her now that the real commitment would be hers. If Oksana had no family, then Galina would make her a member of her own.

After much persuasion from Viktor, Galina, and another coach, Valentine Nicolaj, 14-year-old Oksana Baiul moved to Odessa. She packed

Clowning around on the ice with Oksana is fellow Ukranian Viktor Petrenko, who became her surrogate big brother when she moved to Odessa to train with Coach Galina Zmievskaya.

everything she owned into one suitcase, boarded a train by herself, and left Dnepropetrovsk and Slavik and her memories behind in search of a new life.

In Odessa Oksana became part of a new family. She shared a bedroom with Galina's 12-year-old daughter, Galya, and was treated like a member of the family. Oksana blossomed under such care.

Viktor became her new big brother. He bought her the first new skates she ever owned. With Galina's coaching and Viktor's influence and protective advice, Oksana could do nothing but thrive. She was like a dry, thirsty plant that was finally watered into bloom.

Oksana was shocked the first time she entered the Odessa skating rink. The ice was soft and slushy with little hills and rough edges, extremely dangerous conditions for skating. It was covered with green algae. There was no working Zamboni (the machine that sweeps the ice clean), so Oksana and the other skaters would clean the ice themselves with shovels and brooms. The toilets were missing their seats. Sometimes the power shut down, but the skaters would keep practicing—in the freezing dark. And conditions worsened by the day.

But Oksana was so focused and so thrilled with the professional and personal attention she received that she didn't care how bad conditions were. Life was kind to her again. She and all the other skaters shoveled and swept up the messes on the rink and laughed about it.

Galina was a tough coach but a good one, thrilled to have such a gifted and willing student on her hands. She taught Oksana right away how to put more footwork into her programs. She worked Oksana until the girl was gasping for breath.

Galina also taught Oksana how to contort herself gracefully into what would become her signature spin. In this unique move Oksana stretched her right arm over her shoulder to grab hold of her left skate behind her head, making a circle of her upper body. It was a difficult, painful pose to hold, and she had to learn to add speed to it. But it was beautiful to watch.

Galina believed that a skater could be expressive and artful. She taught Oksana to make every gesture a thing of beauty, down to the wave of her hand. Oksana was enrolled in ballet to learn how to express story and emotion through physical movement. She was a natural for it, and she effectively transferred what she learned in ballet to the ice.

Away from the ice, Galina's home became a precious space to Oksana. The three-room apartment in a high-rise building that sat between a prison and a cemetery was home to Oksana, Galina and her husband, Galina's mother, young Galya, Nina (soon to be Viktor's wife), a dog, a goldfish, and a cockatoo that screamed the Russian word for "hello" whenever the phone rang.

Oksana and Galya plastered pictures and needlepoint on the walls of their bedroom where their twin beds sat footboard to footboard. They both loved chocolate, collected teddy bears, and danced around the apartment to rap songs from the radio. Oksana also loved going to church with Galina's mother. It was almost like having a new babushka to teach her prayers and tell her stories.

In December 1992 Oksana entered the Ukrainian National Championship. Her short program was a flamenco routine that highlighted her natural dance instincts and hard work. For this she wore black with lots of fringe.

She performed the long program to a medley of Broadway tunes, wearing a bright blue costume trimmed in gold. She won first place.

This qualified Oksana to represent Ukraine at the European Championships in Helsinki, Finland, in January 1993. On New Year's Day, however, Coach Galina had a heart attack. The doctors assured Oksana that Galina would be just fine, but Oksana would not leave Galina's hospital bedside. She couldn't bear the thought of losing her second mother and coach. Beside herself with worry, she told Galina she would not compete in the European Championships.

But Galina would have none of that. She reminded Oksana of all their hard work and success. She reminded her that the doctors said she would be well again soon. Then she scolded, pointing out that Oksana's mother would want her to perform.

Oksana knew this was true, and she changed her mind. She packed her costumes and took her flamenco and Broadway programs to Helsinki, where she won over the audience, who cheered wildly, and brought home the silver medal.

The European skating world buzzed, wondering who this little skater was and why they had never heard of her before. It was an amazing feat for someone so young to win a silver medal against such competition.

Her victory made her eligible to perform at the World Championships in Prague. At that competition, while trying to adjust to skating on new skates, she ran into the boards around the rink, injuring a disk in her back. The doctors checked her over and gave her treatments, but her back still hurt her. So she competed in pain against great skaters such as Surya Bonaly, Chen Lu, and Nancy Kerrigan. In spite of great

Despite injuries and tough competition from skaters like Surya Bonaly, Chen Lu, and Nancy Kerrigan at the 1993 Worlds in Prague, Oksana, shown flying through the air, became the youngest person to win the Worlds in over half a century.

odds against her, Oksana won the gold medal, the youngest skater to win the World Championship since 1927.

Reporters flocked around Oksana while she wept, partly from pain, partly from joy. "My tears are God's kisses from my mother in heaven," she told them.

Oksana flew back to Ukraine to prepare for the next skating adventure—the Campbell Soup Tour of World Figure Skating Champions. At 15 Oksana traveled for the first time to the United States and performed in over 40 cities with Viktor and many of her skating idols such as Jill Trenary and Brian Boitano.

It was a heady experience to live in celebrity luxury for a change. Oksana enjoyed shopping at the malls, eating new foods, and signing autographs. She spoke no English, so Viktor kept his brotherly eye on her.

On the tour she experienced more stage fright than she'd ever felt, so she pictured Slavik in her mind and skated for him. She was much loved on the tour because she had already developed a taste for playing to an audience. She was a consummate performer, able to convey feelings on ice with all the sensitivity of a professional dancer or actor.

When the tour ended, Oksana and Galina flew to Sun Valley, Idaho, for a competition. There, while taking a walk, they saw swans in a pond, and Oksana mentioned to her coach how much her mother had wanted her to skate to *Swan Lake*.

Galina smiled. The time had come to do that very thing, she told her, and the two began strategizing a new program to the strains of *Swan Lake*.

Back home, the new *Swan Lake* short program was choreographed by Oksana's ballet teacher, Nina Stoyan, and Galina. Nina insisted, against Galina's protests, that Oksana do part of the program tiptoeing on the toes of her blades so that she would look like a ballet dancer dancing in toe shoes. These were physically painful moves, and Oksana had to learn to work through the cramping in her feet for weeks. But she did it, and the results were breathtaking and unique.

That fall Oksana competed in Skate America, but her performance was unimpressive. Then she placed second at the Nation's Cup competition in Germany. After the new year, she competed in the 1994 European Championships in Copenhagen, Denmark, where she won the silver medal once again.

All these were excellent experiences for the young skater, and the world started watching her. She went to the 1994 Olympics with confidence, but did not expect the triumphant performance that made her a hero in her native country. Overcoming an accident and her chronic back pain, she overwhelmed the audience and brought the Ukraine its first gold medal.

CHANGES

Back home in the Ukraine after the Olympics, Oksana's countrymen were thrilled with their hometown girl. A crowd waited for her plane to land in Kiev, and as she deplaned, flowers and praises were heaped upon her. The proud but struggling young nation saw Oksana as a symbol of good things to come. They treated her like a star.

Ukraine's President Kravchuk presented her with more money than she could imagine—the equivalent of $15,000. In the United States, most people earn much more than that amount in a year. But people in the Ukraine usually earn about $20 per month.

Then President Kravchuk asked Oksana and Viktor Petrenko to accompany him to the United States to dine with President Clinton

Following her Olympic victory in 1994, Oksana Baiul and Viktor Petrenko accompanied Ukrainian president Kravchuk to the White House for a dinner with U.S. president Bill Clinton.

and other celebrities at the White House. She dressed in an elegant black dress and heels and had a wonderful time. President Clinton summed up Oksana's mystique by saying her face had an "ageless" look about it. Deep in her heart, Oksana knew her mother was there in spirit.

From the beginning America fell in love with Oksana. Americans have always loved a rags-to-riches story, and they adored the spirited Ukrainian who skated her way to the top on guts and raw talent. Newscaster Barbara Walters named Oksana one of her "Ten Most Interesting People of 1994." The open arms of Americans helped Oksana and her new family make a very difficult decision.

Back in the Ukraine, conditions were getting worse, despite the Ukrainians' belief that life would improve some day. As Oksana began training in Odessa for the Tour of Champions, skating conditions at the rink were nearly impossible. The rink was still drafty, dark, and in disrepair, only worse than before. But the national shortages affected everything else in daily life, and it was probably the lack of good medical care that ultimately made the skaters decide to leave the Ukraine.

Although Oksana, Viktor, and Galina loved their home country, it was now impossible even to get a clean bed in a hospital. The medical facilities were not sterile, and basic procedural tools—needles, medicines, and simple bandages—were missing. Everyone stockpiled whatever they could of these items in their homes, hoping there would be no emergencies. This clearly was a problem for Oksana, an athlete with a troublesome back injury that continued to flare.

Even the airport had shortages. Sometimes there wasn't enough jet fuel to fly out of Odessa.

It would be impossible to tour under such conditions. In some ways, the decision to move was easy for the Ukrainians. The training conditions would be superior, and the skaters could get all the good medical attention they needed. On the other hand, moving to America meant leaving loved ones and their own proud, fledgling nation. In particular for Oksana, it meant leaving Slavik. But they all agreed that their careers and their health could not wait for Ukraine to improve.

An American skating coach named Bob Young had built a multimillion-dollar skating rink in Simsbury, Connecticut, with two rinks, a weight room, and a ballet room. Years before, Galina and her family had been hospitable to Young when he was visiting the Soviet Union, and he never forgot it. Now he invited Galina

The collapse of the Soviet Union and independence in the Ukraine brought a new set of hardships to Ukrainians as the country struggled to print its own currency and rebuild its infrastructure. Shoppers were frequently faced with empty shelves like these in a Kiev store.

Oksana played Clara in an on-ice version of the Nutcracker, *performed here by the New York City Ballet.*

and her skaters to come to Connecticut to train and to live. They accepted his offer.

Oksana decided to turn professional. For the first time in her life, Oksana could work and make money. She was offered product sponsorships besides the skating. She chose not to train for the 1998 Olympics, but developed new entertaining programs instead.

The landscape of Connecticut reminded Oksana of Ukraine. She took a handful of Ukraine soil with her, mixed it into the Connecticut soil, and vowed to make a new life in her new country. Oksana began training for professional performances and took lessons in English. She trained in the rink while fans watched. She worked out in the weight room and at the ballet barre. In her spare time, she chased after all the things her money could buy like a child turned loose in a candy shop for the first time. Oksana shopped and shopped, scooping up makeup and teddy bears. She moved into a condo next door to Galina and filled it with the stuffed animals her fans gave her and one real animal—a cocker spaniel named Rudik.

Finally the abandoned child was getting all the attention she could stand. And Oksana dearly loved attention. She enjoyed signing autographs when she shopped, and sitting for makeovers in department stores while a crowd watched.

As always, there was the thrill of performance. Oksana's smile beamed at her audience of strangers like a lighthouse in fog, and her smile was absolutely genuine. Performing was everything she ever hoped it would be.

In America, yet another dream came true for Oksana—she performed in the *Nutcracker*. Joining Brian Boitano in "Nutcracker on Ice," Oksana played Clara and relished every minute of it. She remembered her babushka and grandfather taking her to see this ballet performed when she was a little girl in Dnepropetrovsk. She had wanted so badly to dance in it, and she remembered chattering about it all the time around the apartment.

Over the years, Oksana's body had been maturing. She grew taller and fuller. She no longer looked like a waif. Some coaches get nervous when this happens. But Galina knew it was natural, and she decided to work with it. She presented her young charge with a sketch of a costume that Oksana would wear to skate a program with an Arabian theme. It was a harem girl outfit with gauzy pantaloons slit up the side and a spangled bikini top. This meant her midriff would be bare. But Galina reminded her, "You are not a little girl anymore. It is time to grow up. It is time to try something new."

Oksana Baiul smiles as she accepts the Inspirational Award at the Jim Thorpe Pro Sports Awards in July of 1994.

Oksana gulped and agreed. She wore the costume and somehow looked both exotic and elegant. She sometimes used a genie lamp for a prop. She learned new moves, and, as usual, she found her coach to be right. Audiences were mesmerized. Her Arabian program was a hit.

From then on, Galina spotlighted Oksana's creativity, her exotic beauty, and her natural ease. Oksana tried the programs out on adoring audiences and loved every minute of it.

In November 1995, Oksana turned 18. She had everything money could buy. She was young, beautiful, and famous. She lived in a mansion, drove a Mercedes, and was adored all over the world.

But something was still missing. No matter how mature she may have seemed and how much money she earned, Oksana was still just a teenager, without parents. She still felt alone in the world, and all the adulation on earth could not fill the void deep inside her. She was restless and anxious in her soul. The loneliness that had haunted her since childhood began to catch up to her.

A New Birthday

On November 20, 1995, a few days after Oksana's 18th birthday, she received a phone call from her good friend and fellow skater, Ekaterina Gordeeva. While training for an ice show in Lake Placid, Ekaterina's husband and skating partner, Sergei Grinkov, had suffered a massive heart attack and died on the ice. He was only 28 years old.

Oksana was stunned. Sergei was her neighbor in Simsbury and he treated her like his kid sister. She hurt badly for Ekaterina. And then she felt abandoned again. It brought back the pain of all the deaths and desertions she had experienced in her life. At a press conference in Simsbury regarding Sergei's death, she moaned, "God, why do you take from me such good people?"

Oksana proudly holds a copy of her autobiography, Oksana: My Own Story, *published in 1997.*

Together with Bob Young, director of the International Skating Center in Simsbury, Connecticut, Oksana and her coach express their sympathy to Sergei Grinkov's family. Oksana was shocked by Sergei's sudden death in 1995.

Oksana flew to Sergei's funeral in Moscow, where skaters like Scott Hamilton, Paul Wylie, and many others had flown in from around the world to express their sorrow and sympathy to Ekaterina and her family.

When she returned to the U.S., Oksana performed at the Riders Ladies final in Boston. In her third program, she changed her performance and dedicated it to Sergei. She wore a black costume to suggest mourning and skated dramatically to Madonna's song, "You'll See." She did not achieve technical excellence in this performance, but her movements were fluid and meaningful. She let her emotions out on the ice. At the end of the program, she curled up on the ice, weeping, and there was not a dry eye in the house.

This performance put Oksana in fourth place when she probably would have placed higher had she not been so overcome with grief while performing. It made the performance a controversial one. Some said she was unprofessional; some said she was in no emotional shape to be performing; some said she was a true artist. But all agreed that it was an unforgettable tribute to her friend and former countryman.

After Sergei's death, Oksana continued to live as if she were making up for lost time. Sergei's death at such a young age seemed to increase her restlessness. Fame, which had been such great fun at first, became more difficult as she continued to deal with her new-found freedom.

Added to her inner turmoil, Oksana's body continued to change. She took some time away from the ice, withdrawing from several 1996 competitions. During this time she grew four inches and gained 20 pounds. This made training again much more challenging and frustrating. Skating was the only thing she knew how to do, the only love of her life, but now she felt clumsy doing it. Old back and ankle injuries further compounded her skating problems, and Oksana began skipping practices. Though she continued to skate and to perform, she never won another competition through 1998.

The International Skating Union had given professional skaters like Oksana a chance to return to amateur status and compete in the 1998 Olympic Games. Though Ukrainian officials wanted Oksana to compete in the '98 Olympics, she chose to remain professional and

Oksana is escorted from court by her lawyer in 1997. Newfound money and freedom in the U.S. caused Oksana to put partying and socializing above her skating practice. After a car accident in 1997 and her subsequent arrest on drunk driving charges, Oskana pledged to stop drinking and turn her life around.

enjoy her life as it was, rather than return to the rigors of Olympic training. But without intense training, there was a void in Oksana's life she could not fill.

Eventually, floundering without rules or family to check her behavior, Oksana ran wild. For the next year, she partied, dancing the night away in clubs and drinking alcohol. But she was not having fun, she later reported. "It was horrible. I had a gold medal. Millions. Too much too soon." Oksana had achieved her life goal already, and now she needed something else to live for and to put meaning into her life.

By her 19th birthday, Oksana's drinking was heavy, and in January 1997, while intoxicated, she wrapped her green Mercedes around a tree. She had a passenger in the car, a Russian skater, and both of them sustained minor injuries—Oksana had a mild concussion and a scalp wound that required 14 stitches, and her passenger broke his finger.

When Oksana saw all the blood in the car she began to cry. She realized that she could have been killed and she could have killed someone else as well. She felt the presence of her mother, and she believed Marina had been watching over her as a guardian angel. It was clear to her that her own actions had caused the accident. She had turned into a perpetual drunk and been reckless enough to get behind the wheel of a car.

When Oksana woke up sore and sober with stitches in her head, she vowed never to touch alcohol again. The press attacked Oksana. They had loved her, but now they turned on her. News of her arrest on drunk driving charges flooded the papers. But the negative press did not bother her as much as it might have before the accident, because Oksana now was busy taking control of the direction of her life.

Since she had broken the law and been arrested, Oksana had to go to court, where she was ordered to get alcohol counseling. She enrolled in an alcohol awareness program and performed community service work to help teach others about the dangers of drunk driving. Oksana freely told reporters that now she knew she was an alcoholic and that she felt reborn, having escaped what could easily have been death. She named January 12, the day of the accident, her new "birthday."

Just weeks after her car accident, Oksana skates with other professionals at a Jimmy Fund event in Boston to raise money for the charity.

In the following year, Oksana slowed down and listened to the sadness in her soul instead of running from it. She went on to seek psychological help for the many troubles and insecurities she had accumulated over the years and kept buried. She knew she could no longer skate them away.

The self-examination also turned out to be helpful in the writing of her autobiography, *Oksana: My Own Story.* The book was published in 1997, and promoting it turned out to be a positive thing for the skater in the middle of a life transition.

Perhaps as part of starting over, Oksana hired a new coach—Sara Kawahara—and began rebuilding her career. She also left her big lonely house and moved to Boston, Massachusetts.

In 1998 Oksana skated with the star-studded Campbell Soup Champions on Ice tour, alongside Tara Lipinski, Michelle Kwan, Surya Bonaly, and Nicole Bobek. Baiul was one of the crowd's favorites in the ice show, which was her sixth professional ice tour.

She began to skate with renewed enthusiasm, sometimes performing a solo in which she skated the life cycle of a flower. In this performance, "I come up from underground and become full bloom," she explained.

She was really skating the story of her own life. Oksana had experienced many tragedies and uprootings in her life, but somehow, each time she managed to go on and succeed. Oksana Baiul learned to accept her blessings alongside her sadnesses, as if she was blooming once again in new ways.

In the spring of 1998, however, Oksana learned that her battle with alcoholism was not over. After a renewed struggle with heavy drinking, she checked into an alcoholism treatment center. Her fans hope that the determination and strength that saw Oksana through the hardships of her early life will help her land on her feet again, and return to the elegant, expressive skating that has won the hearts of millions.

"I just want to build a new Oksana," she has said. "I'm getting there."

CHRONOLOGY

1977   Oksana Baiul born November 16 in the Ukrainian town of Dnepropetrovsk to Marina and Sergei Baiul.

1979   Father abandons the family.

1980   Oksana's grandfather gives her her first ice skates.

1985   Stanislav Korytek becomes Oksana's coach.

1986   Oksana learns the triple Lutz at the age of nine. Chernobyl nuclear disaster strikes; all of the Soviet Union is affected.

1987   Oksana's grandfather dies.

1988   Oksana watches her first Olympics on TV.

1989   Oksana's grandmother dies.

1991   Oksana's mother dies of cancer.

1992   Moves to Odessa to train and live with coach Galina Zmievskaya.

1993   Wins gold in the World Championships in Prague.

1994   Wins gold medal in the Olympics.

1995   Turns professional and moves to Simsbury, Connecticut.

FURTHER READING

Baiul, Oksana. *Oksana: My Own Story.* New York: Random House, 1997.

Gordeeva, Ekatarina, and E. M. Swift. *My Sergei: A Love Story.*
New York: Warner Books, 1996.

Shaughnessy, Linda. *Oksana Baiul: Rhapsody on Ice.* New Jersey:
Crestwood House, 1998.

ABOUT THE AUTHOR

Lonnie Hull DuPont lives in Ann Arbor, Michigan, with her husband, Joe. She edits books of all kinds. She is also a poet and the author of a biography about Harriet Tubman for young readers.

GLOSSARY

AXEL: a jump named for its inventor, Axel Paulsen. The Axel is the only jump launched while skating forward. A skater takes off from the forward outside skate edge and lands on the opposite foot on a back outside edge. A double Axel is the same jump with two and a half mid-air rotations. A triple Axel, achieved for the first time in 1978, requires three and a half mid-air rotations.

CAMEL: a skating spin performed with one leg extended back; the camel is called a flying camel when a skater jumps into the spin.

CROSSOVER: performed when a skater crosses his or her stride; a crossover tends to increase a skater's speed.

DEATH SPIRAL: a pairs figure skating move in which the man pivots and spins the woman in a circle around him with one hand while her arched body spirals down until it is almost parallel to the ice.

FLIP: a jump made by sticking the blade pick into the ice, revolving, and then landing on the back outside edge of the toe-assisting foot; the triple flip is the same jump with three revolutions.

FOOTWORK: any series of turns, steps, hops, and crossovers done at high speed.

LIFTS: pairs moves in which the man holds the woman up in a ballet-like position over his head; variations on lifts include the star lift, in which the woman holds both her arms in the air, and the one-armed lift, in which the man supports the woman with only one arm.

LOOP: a jump in which the skater takes off and lands on the same back outside edge.

LUTZ: a jump named for its creator, Alois Lutz. For the Lutz, a skater takes off on a back outside edge, revolves, and then lands on a back outside edge. When a skater revolves three times in the air, the jump is called a triple Lutz.

SALCHOW: a jump named after Swedish skater Ulrich Salchow. For the Salchow, a skater makes a long glide backward and then takes off on the outside edge of one skate, with a boost from the toe of the opposite skate. After revolving, the skater lands on the outside edge of the boosting skate. A double Salchow has two rotations; a triple Salchow requires three full rotations while in the air.

SPIN: a skater performs a spin by rotating from one fixed point; when skaters spin, they move so fast their image becomes blurred.

SIT SPIN: a spin in which the skater crouches down, balanced on one leg while the other extends; often a skater will pull up out of a sit spin to a standing spin position.

SPREAD-EAGLE: a move in which a skater glides on two feet, with the lead foot on a forward edge and the trail foot on the same edge, only backward.

TOE LOOP: a jump launched off the toe pick of the free foot in which a skater completes one rotation and lands on the back outside edge of the same foot. The toe pick can launch the skater to a great height; hence, a double toe loop has two mid-air rotations, and a triple toe loop has three.

THROWS: pairs moves in which the man throws the woman into the air, where she spins two or three times before landing on one foot.

INDEX